Winter

Nicola Baxter

Illustrated by Kim Woolley

W

FRANKLIN WATTS

LONDON · NEW YORK · SYDNEY

During the autumn the days grow shorter and the weather gets colder.
Slowly winter arrives.

Now try this

Do you think the photograph on the next page was taken in the autumn or the winter?

Can you be really sure?

The winter sun is not very hot.
We need to wear warm clothes
when it is cold outside.

Now try this

Some people put their summer clothes away when the
weather gets colder. Which of these clothes might
you wear in the winter?

Running and playing keeps you warm too. But you can tell that it is cold if your breath makes little clouds in front of your face.

Try this later

On a cold day, blow on to the window pane.
The cold glass will turn your breath
into tiny drops of water.
The same thing happens to your breath
in the air outdoors on a very cold day.

Sometimes it is so cold outside that water freezes and turns into ice. Putting grit or salt on roads and paths helps to stop people sliding.

8

When it is cold, rain is frozen
as it falls from the clouds.
It may fall as little lumps of ice,
called hail, or as snowflakes.

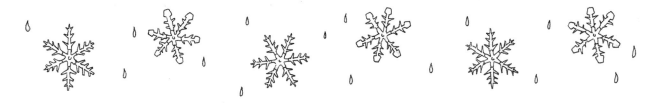

Try this later

Under a microscope, all snowflakes have
six sides and each one is different.
Draw round a plate on white paper
and cut out the circle.
Ask a grown-up to help you follow these
steps to make your own snowflake.

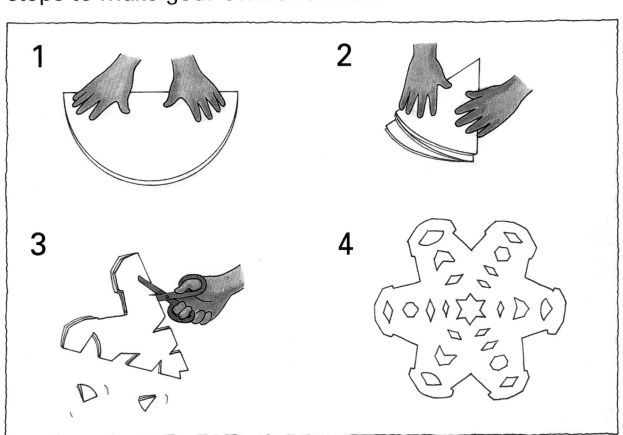

If the weather is very cold, the ground may be covered with snow all winter.

Some sports and games can only be played when it is very cold.

When you have been outside
in the cold, hot food and drinks
taste good and warm you up.

Farmers need to feed their animals extra food to keep them going through the winter.

It is sometimes hard for wild birds and
animals to find food.
When ponds and puddles are frozen,
it is difficult to find water to drink, too.

16

Try this too

At winter celebrations, candles and lights cheer up the cold, dark days and remind people that the winter can be a time of new beginnings too.

For many people, the beginning of a new year is celebrated in the winter.

Try this later
Ask a grown-up to help you make
a calendar of the year.
Draw or cut out pictures for each month
and be sure to mark the times that
are special to you each year.

Winter seems to last a long time.
But even before winter is over,
the first signs of spring can be seen.

Index

© 1996 Franklin Watts

Franklin Watts
96 Leonard Street
London
EC2A 4RH

Franklin Watts Australia
14 Mars Road
Lane Cove
NSW 2066

ISBN: 0 7496 2340 3

Dewey Decimal Classification
Number 574.5

A CIP catalogue record for this
book is available from the British
Library.

Editor: Sarah Ridley
Designer: Kirstie Billingham
Picture researcher: Sarah Moule

Printed in Malaysia

Acknowledgements: the
publishers would like to thank
Carol Olivier and Kenmont Primary
School for their help with the
cover for this book.

Photographs: Bubbles 5, 6; Bruce
Coleman Ltd 9, 23; James Davis Travel
Photography 13; Robert Harding
Picture Library 10; Peter Millard
(cover); Natural History Photographic
Agency 3, 16; Oxford Scientific Films
15; Trip 18, 21.